ACOUSTIA

BAR CHORDS IN 5 DAYS

INSTRUCTED BY ANDREW SEGUIN

1ST EDITION

BAR CHORDS IN 5 DAYS
VIDEO COURSE

Here at Acoustia, our programs also include step-by-step video lessons. **You can purchase the follow along video lessons at the following link:**

WWW.ACOUSTIA.COM/BAR-CHORDS-IN-5-DAYS

video lessons not included with workbook

BIOGRAPHY

Andrew Seguin is the founder Acoustia™. The online guitar school disrupting traditional guitar lessons. With it's step-by-step, easy to follow systems.

Andrew has been playing guitar since the age of 8. After trying to learn from YouTube lessons and failing, he decided to try something different and get a teacher. This teacher taught him the ins and outs of guitar in a step-by-step way. The way that the Acoustia™ programs are now structured.

He became obsessed with fingerstyle and classical guitar, and began playing his first gigs at the age of 14. He's received hundreds of thousands of views on his fingerstyle music videos, and even has a guitar gold medal from the Royal Conservatory of Music for Classical Guitar. Andrew has over 10,000+ hours of guitar experience in Fingerstyle & Classical Guitar and is a certified instructor.

Andrew founded Acoustia to create an easier, better way to learn guitar. One that didn't cost thousands of dollars, and was step-by-step and easy. Just like he learned. With proven systems that you can follow, instead of doing it all yourself. Acoustia currently has hundreds of students, and has helped tens of thousands worldwide get better at different aspects of their guitar player. Acoustia is currently the online leader in Acoustic guitar lessons. With easy to follow programs like *Bar Chords in 5 Days*. Andrew works on becoming the best guitar play he can, and creating the top guitar programs.

INTRODUCTION

Welcome! I want to first congratulate you on joining *Bar Chords in 5 Days*. Throughout my years as a teacher, a lot of people have mentioned their struggles with bar chords to me. So I wanted to create an easy program with the lessons I've shared with them, aswell as some new exercises to get better at them. We'll go through it a lot in the program, but one of the easiest fixes for cleaner bar chords is just fixing your guitar hand position. We will go over that more in the program.

Depending on your purchase. I also would recommend that you follow along with the video course aswell. That's going to help you better understand the lessons, and will definitely help with your learning. If you have any problems accessing the program, then just send us an email. Although, if you're more of a reader, this workbook will still help you learn.

I also wanted to mention that you don't need to go through this program in exactly 5 days. If you're completely new to bar chords, I'd recommend taking it slow so you can understand the concepts before moving on. That being said, if you have some experience in bar chords and just want to get better, you'll be able to go through this program much faster. It all just depends on how quickly you can go through the exercises. Take your time, and go as you feel.

We start the program by going through basic bar chords, and then by the end go over all of the different shapes. There's also a bonus lesson that we added at the end of the program called ''7th chords''. This just showcases some rare 7th bar chords that you may see. This lesson was more of a bonus that we added on, as on the rare occasion you'll see some 7th chords. But I'd recommend at the end to check that out as it can help you later on.

You don't have to obsess over the exercises in the program. I just recommend going through them until you can play the notes and bar chords consistently clean. There's no specific amount of time you need to practice them, but I'd just say till you feel comfortable. That may be in minutes, hours, or days. But if you need to split up the exercises over a few days that OK, just be consistent.

The main message I will leave you with is this. Just be consistent! The most successful guitar players are usually the ones who just do it everyday. Even if that's just 5 minutes when you get a chance. Stay consistent, go through the exercises, follow the lessons and you'll get results.

Andrew Seguin

TABLE OF CONTENTS

DAY 1 - HALF BARING (PART 1)

Welcome to Day 1 of Bar Chords in 5 Days. Throughout this program, I'm going to be sharing with you my top tips, exercises and methods to get you playing clean bar chords fast. Maybe you've struggled to play bar chords in the past, or have always wanted to. Either way this will help you.

A lot of people think that the harder they press on their guitar, the cleaner the sound will be. This ISN'T true. Infact, the first thing we'll be going over is guitar position. This is because sometimes the cause of bar chord struggle is bad position. After that, the next step is playing easy bar chords, and then difficult ones. **Let's get into it...**

GUITAR POSITION

When someone comes to me and they have a hard time playing bar chords, the first thing I have a look at is there position. A lot of times this is what causes them to have a hard time playing the bar chords. If you have bad guitar position, you will have a difficult time playing bar chords.

There are 4 main keys to your position:

1. Thumb Behind The Neck
Having your thumb behind the neck gives your fingers more room to hit the proper notes. A lot of people have the habit of having their thumb hang over the neck of their guitar.

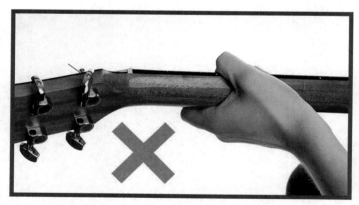

Take a look at the two photos to the right. The first one would be a bad position, because of the thumb placement. But the second one where the thumb is flat behind the neck is perfect. Make sure to always keep your thumb behind the neck. **This will help with your bar chords.**

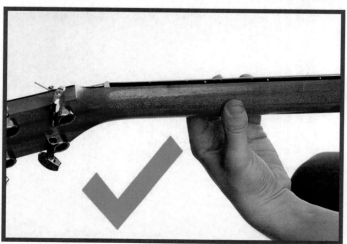

2. Fingertips Curled

The second step to your guitar position is having your fingertips curled. This is especially important for bar chords. Sometimes guitar players have a habit of laying their left hand fingers flat because it's easier.

Take a look at the photos on the right. When your fingers are flat, it can cause a lot of buzzing. Work over time on curling your fingertips when you try to play bar chords. Like the second photo It makes it easier to hit the specific frets. **This may be the most important part to your position for bar chords. Having your fingertips curled will help bar chords sound clean.**

3. Horizontal Finger Placement

The third step to your guitar position is having your left hand fingers laying horizontal on the fretboard.

A lot of times guitar plays have the habit of moving their fingers in a vertical way to make it easier to play chords like in the first photo. Although sometimes you'll need to do this, work hard to try to always keep your left hand fingers laying horizontal.

If you've tried to play bar chords in the past but struggled, just adding in these 3 tips may be the solution. Try it out.

4. Wrist Hovering Over Soundhole

The last aspect of your positioning has to do with your right hand. **It's mostly for fingerstyle and classical guitar players,** but it's something to keep in mind for everyone. This is to have your right hand wrist hovering over the soundhole.

A bad habit a lot of Acoustic or Classical guitar players have when they first start, is to have their wrist laying flat on the guitar. **You can see that in Photo 1.** The problem with this is it can lead to wrist problems, and make playing songs hard.

Take a look at the second photo. **This would be a better positioning for your right hand wrist.**

(For Fingerstyle and Classical Players)

Note: These 4 positioning keys are a lot to think about. Don't try to add them all in at once, especially if you have a few of the bad positioning habits I pointed out. Work on adding in one at a time. So first work on Step 1 of your position, and once you have that, then move on to Step 2. Don't overwhelm yourself. **Work on your position one aspect at a time, until you have all the position keys down.**

This also isn't something you will get perfect. More difficult songs and bar chords may require you to move your hand in different ways. I still have to check my position and fix it when I learn new songs. **But always work on getting it better.**

When you are playing bar chords, and it isn't coming out clear or there is buzz. Just check all the aspects of your position. Maybe your thumb is hanging over the neck of your guitar, or maybe your fingertips aren't curled enough. Fix all of them one at a time, and there's a good chance that one of them will make the bar chord sound clean. **Now we are going to start training our hands to play bar chords.**

HALF BARING (PART 1)

Now that you know what good position looks like, we're going to start going through different exercises to train your hand and get you used to playing bar chords.

The first thing that we're going to look at is the half bar, which is easier then the full bar. You may have seen this type of bar if you have tried to play an F chord in the past. It's where instead of your first finger baring all the strings. It will bar all the strings. **Below is a difference between the half bar and full bar.**

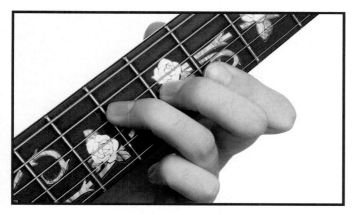

(Example of a Half Bar)

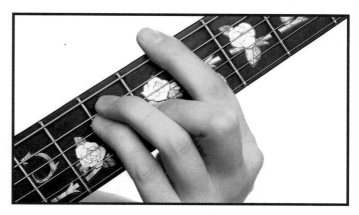

(Example of a Full Bar)

In the first exercise, we are going to play a half bar up the neck. Bar chords up the neck are a little easier then when they are lower because the distance between the frets.

To the right your can see the first chord we are going to be playing in the exercises. Which is an A chord on the 5th fret, using a half bar. To play it, our third finger is placed on the 4th string 7th fret, second finger is placed on the 3rd string 6th fret, and our first finger is bared over both the 1st and second string on the 5th fret.

Take a look at the diagrams on the right. We're going to do a few exercises with this chord to get us started with playing bar chords.

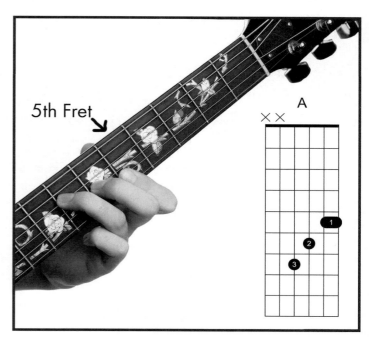

HALF BARING (PART 1)

Instead of just going at it and trying to play this first chord, there's a few exercises that we can do to get started. The first one we'll do is simple. Just lay down the chord. And then play each of the notes separately. Apply pressure to only the note the you are playing.

Look at the tab below. Lay down the half bar A Chord. But don't apply a lot of pressure. Then play each note separate. Apply pressure to only one note at a time. **Do this until the notes come out clean.**

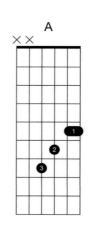
A

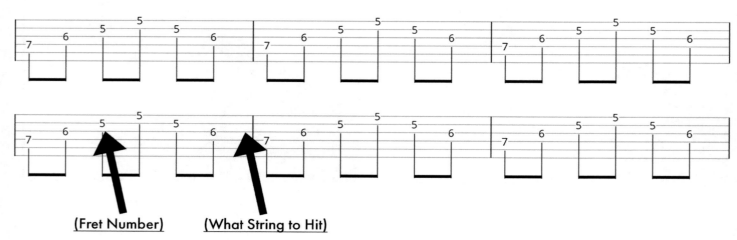

(Fret Number)   (What String to Hit)

If you've never read tab before. It's super simple. The lines are the strings, and the numbers area the frets. The lowest line would be the lowest string, and the highest line would be the highest strings. It's easy once you understand it.

Once you're comfortable with the first exercise, you can move on to the next one. **In this one try to just strum or pluck the half bar chord.** Just lay your chord out (as shown before), and play the full thing. Strum, or pluck it, depending on your style.

Work on getting it as clean as possible with good position.

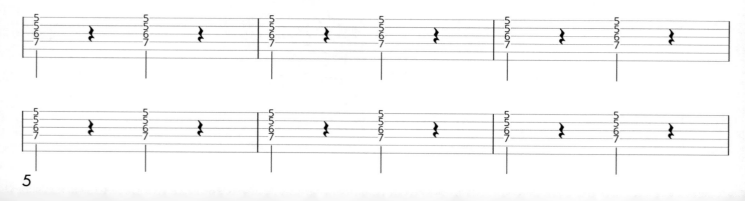

Now we're going to be putting both of the last exercises together.

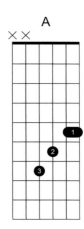

A

In the first one, we looked at putting down the half bar chord, and then playing each of the notes separate. In the second exercise we looked at just playing the chord full. **Now we're going to do both.**

In this last Day 1 Exercise. Start by laying the chord day (shown right), then pluck each note individually. Apply pressure <u>only</u> to the specific note that you're playing at that time.

Once you are comfortable with playing each note individually clean, then strum or pluck the full chord. **Remember to have the bar chord layed down throughout the full exercise, but when you are plucking the notes individually only apply pressure to the note that you are hitting.** Play it until it becomes comfortable.

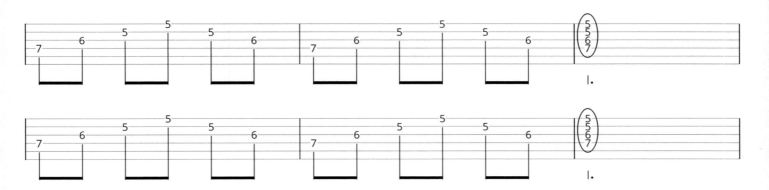

If you are struggling to make the notes clear, take a step back and look at your position. *Is your thumb behind the neck? Are your fingertips curled?* These are all important things that you need to keep in mind while you are going through the exercise.

This is the end of Day 1. Work on practicing the 3 exercises with proper position. It may take some time to get this down. Make sure you are playing the right chord, which is shown in the tab, aswell as on page 4.

<u>Note:</u> There's no time limit to how long it takes to go through these exercises. If they are easy for you, you can move onto the next day. But if you are still struggling, don't be afraid to practice these exercises for a few days before you move on (*just stay consistent everyday*).

HALF BARING (PART 2)

Now we are going to be playing the half bar chord lower on the neck. This makes it a little more difficult because the space between frets is a little more. So make sure that your thumb is behind the neck, and your fingertips are curled.

Here is the chord that we're going to be playing:

As you can see, it's the same pattern but just moved up the neck. The first finger is on the 1st fret of the 1st and 2nd string. The second finger is on the 2nd fret of the 3rd string. And the third finger is on the 3rd fret of the 4th string. **Look at the diagram and picture to understand this new chord.**

Now we are going to be playing the same exercises as Day 1, except with the new positioning of this half bar chord.

The first exercise that we're going to do is lay the half bar chord, and then play each of the notes individually. So lay down the chord, and start from the bottom and hit each note. Only apply pressure to the note you are hitting (don't hold pressure to all the notes). This will help you understand the amount of pressure you need to get the notes sounding out clear. **Try out the exercise below.**

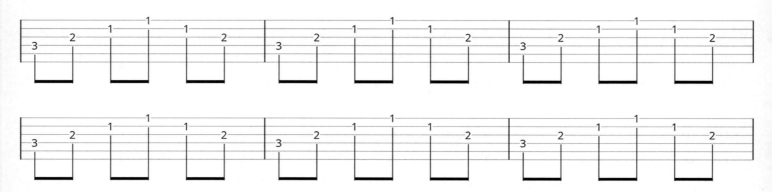

(Watch your position, and make sure it's good)

Once you can start playing the individual notes clean. The next step would be to play the half bar chord full. **That's what we are going to be doing in this next exercise.**

Simply lay out the half bar chord we were looking at (shown right), make sure your position is good (thumb behind neck, fingers curled, fingers horizontal) and then either strum or pluck it out. Make your position better until it sounds clear. Remember, the harder you push doesn't mean the clearer. If your position is good you won't want to push hard. **Try it out below.**

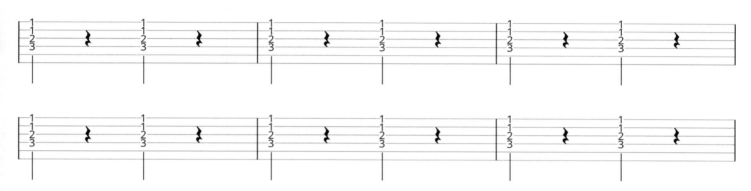

Keep your positioning good, and try to strum or pluck the chord until it sounds clear. If it's buzzing, make sure you are hitting the right notes and your position is good. **Work with it until you can get it sounding clear.**

The next step is going to be putting them both together. Lay the F Chord down (half bar chord down the neck) and pluck each note out individually following the tab. Applying pressure only to the note you are hitting. Then apply pressure to all of the notes, and strum out the full chord. **Follow the tab below.**

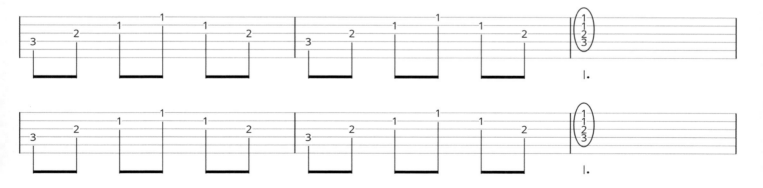

(Move onto Day 3 when you feel you are ready, but **don't rush**)

FULL BARING (PART 1)

The next step is going to be full baring. This is more difficult then half baring. It is a common bar chord throughout a lot of songs . Instead of our first finger baring 2 strings like before, it's going to be barring all 6 strings.

Here is the chord that we are going to be playing:

To start out, we will be doing a full bar chord up the neck. Like I said before, playing it up the neck on the 5th fret will make it easier then playing it on the 1st fret. The chord we are going to be playing the exercises with is an A major chord. **Check it out:**

Your first finger bars all 6 strings, your 2nd is on the 3rd string 6th fret, and your third finger is on the 4th string 7th fret, and your third finger is on the 5th string, 7th fret.

The exercises that we are using to learn full baring are the same as half baring. We are going to lay down the full bar chord shown above. And then hit each note individually, applying pressure only to the note that you are hitting. Still hold the full bar down, but only apply pressure to the note you are hitting.

Go up and down the chord, and only apply pressure to the note you are hitting.

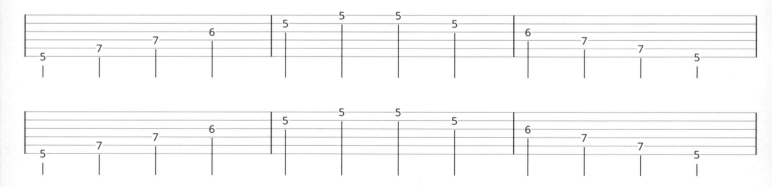

(Practice until it becomes clean)

After you've focused on that, once again the next step would be to strum or pluck the full bar chord. Now instead of just applying pressure to one note at a time, **you will be applying equal pressure to all of the notes.**

Playing a full bar chord like this clean is going to be difficult for the first time. So make sure that your position is good. Don't push as hard as you can, instead focus on your position and apply just enough pressure for it to sound clean. It will be difficult, so practice it a few times, take a break, and practice it again. **Strum or pluck the following full bar chord:**

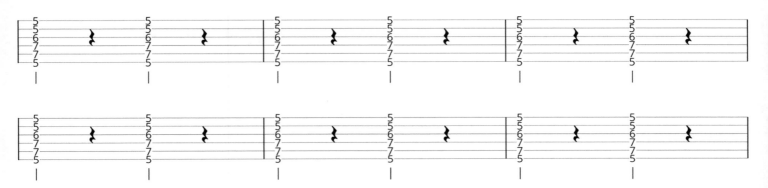

Once you feel like you are comfortable strumming or plucking the bar chord and keeping it clean, the next step is to add both of the exercises together.

In this last exercise, you will lay down the full bar chord, and start out by plucking each of the notes by themselves, applying pressure to each single note making it come out clean. After you've done that, then try to apply equal pressure to the full chord and strum the entire thing out.

If it's not clean, see if there is anything wrong with your position. **Play it below.**

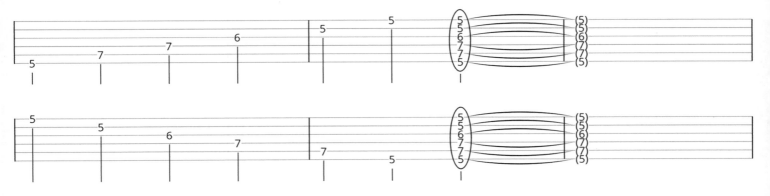

(Move onto Day 4 when you feel you are ready)

FULL BARING (PART 2)

Once you can play a full bar chord higher up the neck, the next step is to play is lower on the neck. As I've mentioned, the lower the barchord the harder it is. This is because of the fret distance. We're going to play a 6th string bar chord on the 1st fret.

Here is the chord that we're going to be playing:

The musical name for the bar chord we going to be playing throughout these exercises is F Major. It is shown in the diagram to the right. To play it: **Have your first finger bar all the strings on the 1th fret, your second finger on the 2nd fret of the 3rd string, fourth finger on the 3rd fret of the 4th string and 3rd finger on the 3rd fret of the 5th string.**

Remember when you are trying to play these bar chords, two keys are to keep your thumb behind the neck, and to curl your fingertips. It will make playing them easier.

We are now going to be playing the same exercise as the previous part, but with the new chord. **Start by placing down the F Major chord. Then pluck each note out, applying pressure only to the note you are hitting. Make sure that every note you are hitting comes out clear.** Go through this as many times as you need to till you get it down. It may take a few minutes, hours, or days before you should move on. **Try it out:**

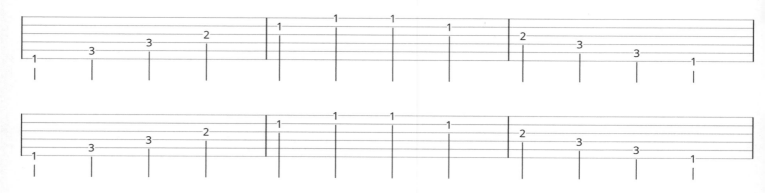

<u>(Hold the full bar down, but only apply pressure to the note you are hitting)</u>

11

The next step to getting full bar chords down is playing them fully together. We're using the same exercise that we have been using throughout.

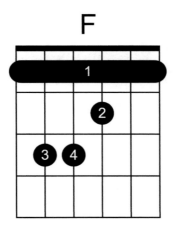

F

Lay the F Major bar chord down, and make sure that you have good position. **Try to apply equal pressure to all of the notes, and then strum.** If it's not sounding clear, look at your position and make sure your fingertips are curled and horizontal (look back at Day 1 for complete position). Try again, and keep strumming until it sounds clear. **Then work on playing it over again until you can consistently play it clean.**

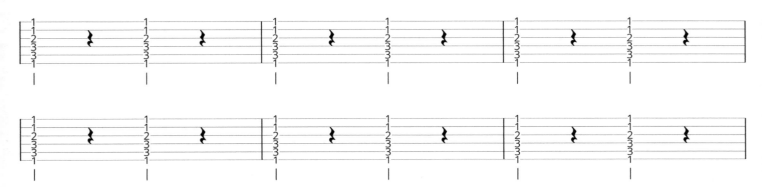

Once you can consistently play it clean. The next step is going to be playing each note clean, and then play all of the notes clean together.

We're using the same exercise as before once again. Start out by laying the F Major bar chord out. And then pluck every note separate, only applying pressure to the one you are plucking. **As shown in the tab below.** Once you've gone through the full chord. Then apply pressure to the full chord and strum it out. The first few times it probably won't be clean. **Keep good position, and practice until you can consistently play it clean.**

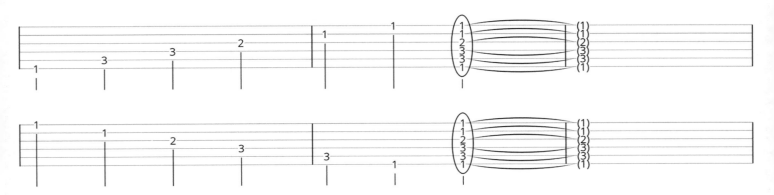

(Move onto Day 5 once you can play this clean. You may need a few days to work on this)

BAR CHORD SHAPES (PART 1)

There's many different bar chord shapes that you'll see. Today we are going to be going over the most common ones, and some exercises to get better at playing them. **Below are the 4 most common bar chord shapes.**

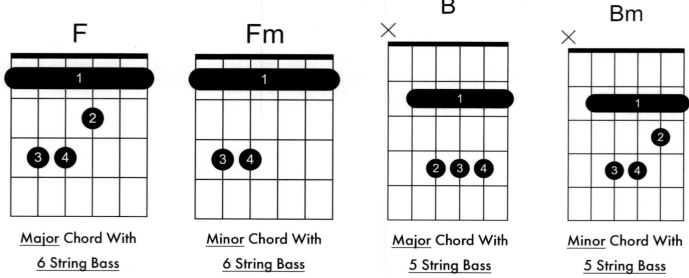

Major Chord With
6 String Bass

Minor Chord With
6 String Bass

Major Chord With
5 String Bass

Minor Chord With
5 String Bass

Now we're going to be going over the 4 different shapes, and exercises to learn them.

1. Major Chord With 6 String Bass

This is the type of bar chord that we've already looked at throughout this program. You can see to the right the exact pattern and fingering. The bass (lowest note) of this chord is on the 6th string, and names the chord. This bar chord pattern can be used to play any major chord on the 6th string.

Below is the exercise that we used to learn to play these bar chords.

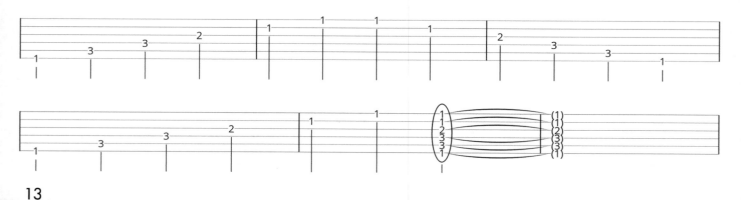

2. Minor Chord With 6 String Bass

The second type of bar chord we will play with a 6 string bass is a minor chord. The only difference between the major and minor bar chord is that we will be lifting out 2nd finger off. You can see to the right, it looks the same, the only difference is we aren't using the second finger note. **You can use the exercise below to get better:**

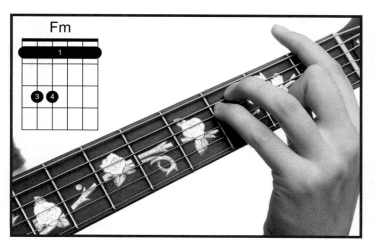

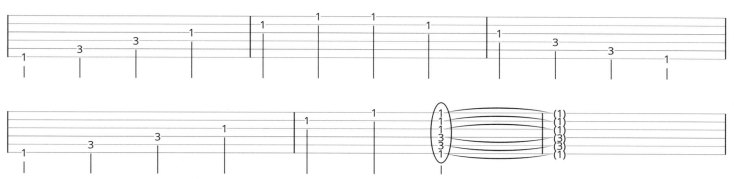

Another exercise you could use to get better at these types of bar chords would to just strum the chord and try to get it as clean as possible. When there's buzzing or it's not clean, it is probably a problem with your position. **Here is an exercise to use below:**

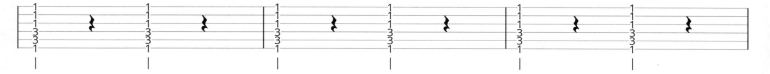

A lot of these exercises will take some time to get down. **Make an effort to practice them a few times a week, even if it's only for a few minutes.** You'll see that everytime you practice them you will get better. You'll also start to develop muscle memory.

Keep an eye on your position (Thumb behind the neck, fingertips curled and horizontal), and try to get everything sounding as clean as possible.

As I've said throughout this book, **position is one of the most important parts when you are trying to play bar chords, after that, practice is what's important.** *Practice, practice, practice.* Just put in the hours practicing the different shapes and exercises, and you will get so much better at them. **Work on getting each note clean by going through the bar chord note-by-note, then play all the notes together.**

3. Major Chord With 5 String Bass

The third type of bar chord that you will see are major chords with a 5 string bass. This is when you will only have to bar 5 strings instead of 6. You can see the shape of these chords on the right. **To get these down, hold down the bar chord shape and go through the exercises we've done.** Work on getting all the notes clean separate, **then play them together:**

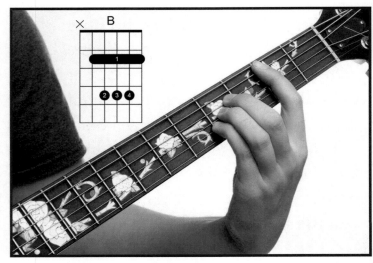

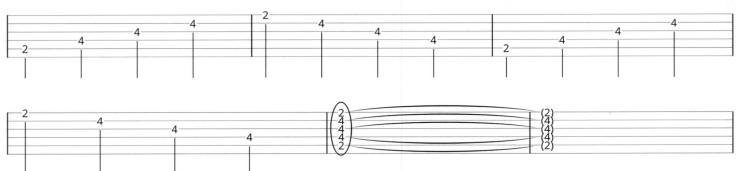

4. Minor Chord With 5 String Bass

You will probably also come across minor bar chords with 5 string bass's. **The only difference between this and the major is the we lower the note on the second string.** If you've worked with basic chords in the past you can see it's just an A-minor chord moved up the fretboard. **Work through the exercises to get the shape down. Always make sure to have good guitar position:**

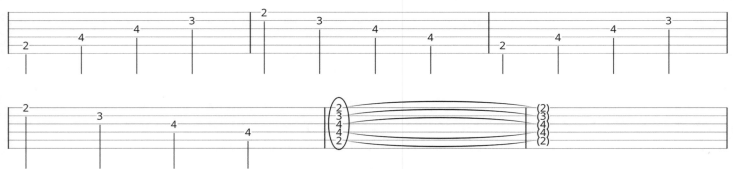

(Try to consistently come back and work on these exercises until they sound clean)

7TH CHORDS (BONUS)

Although it's rare, sometimes you can see 7th Chords in songs. Some 7th chords are also bar chords. **In this bonus lesson, we are going to be talking about 7th bar chords, and the 4 different shapes you can see:**

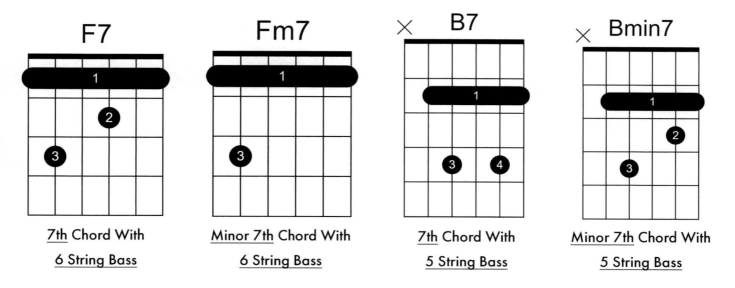

F7	Fm7	B7	Bmin7
7th Chord With 6 String Bass	Minor 7th Chord With 6 String Bass	7th Chord With 5 String Bass	Minor 7th Chord With 5 String Bass

There's four 7th bar chords you'll see (shown above). **We'll start going over each.**

1. 7th Chord With 6 String Bass

This is the first type of 7th chord that you'll see. **You can create a 7th chord with a 6th string bass by simply taking the major version of the chord, and just drop your fourth finger (on 4th string).** This same pattern can work all over the 6th string for different chords by changing the bass.

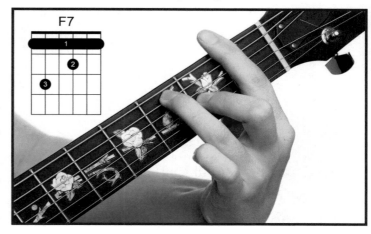

You can use the same exercises to learn 7th chords. Try out the one below:

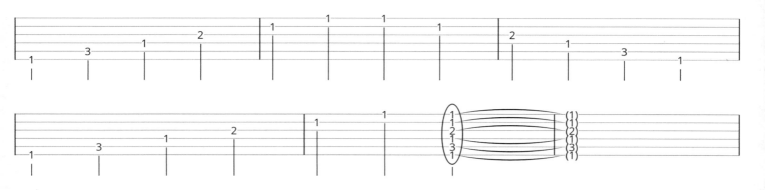

2. Minor 7th Chord With 6 String Bass

Another type of 7th chord with a 6th string bass is a Minor 7th. It's simple to play a minor 7th on the 6th string. **Take the major or minor version of the chord, and drop all of the notes except your third finger (note on 5th string).** Try out the exercise below to work on playing this chord. **Remember to have good position, and watch the tab:**

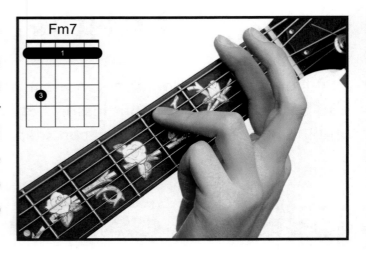

Fm7

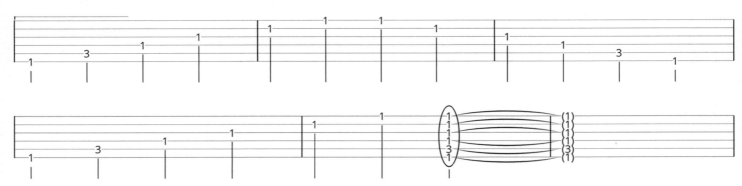

To work on playing these chords clean, use the same exercises that we went over in the previous lesson. Work on first isolating each note and playing them clean, and then try to strum or pluck the full chord together. **Here is the second part of the exercise:**

These exercises will take time to get down. The important thing is that you are consistent. A good idea would be to practice a few bar chords with these exercises as a warmup. Practicing them for only a few minutes a day will make them sound more clean.

If you're struggling to keep them clean, make sure that:

1. Your thumb is behind the neck
2. Your fingertips are curled
3. Your fingers are horizontal and not all over the place

These should really help make your playing sound more clean.

3. 7th Chord With 5 String Bass

The third type of 7th bar chord you may see is a 7th Chord with a 5th string bass. **To play this chord, just take the major version of the chord and play it without using a finger on the 3rd string.** You just have to bar the 5 strings with your 1st finger, and then use your 3rd and 4th finger two frets down on the 4th and 2nd string. **Below is an exercise to use to learn the chord:**

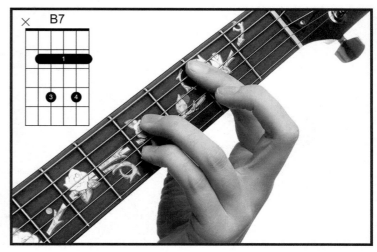

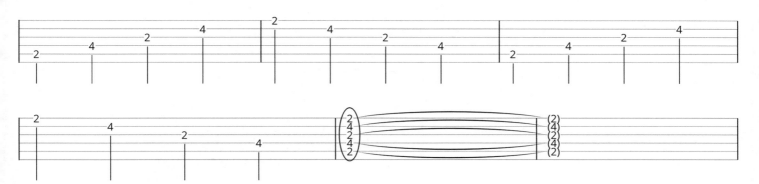

4. Minor 7th Chord With 5 String Bass

The Minor 7th chords is very rare in songs, but you may come across it from time to time. **To play it, take the minor version of the chord, and take off your 2nd and 4th finger. So the only finger you have down besides the bar is your 3rd finger on the 4th string.** You can see a diagram of it to the right. **Once again, work through the exercise below to learn the chord:**

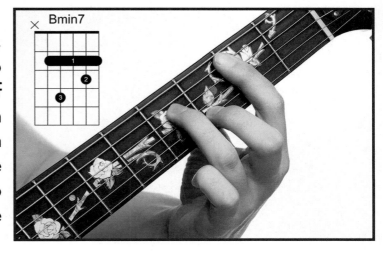

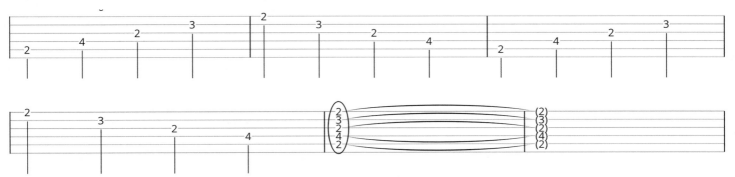

<u>(Take it slow first, make sure all the notes are clean, and then play the full bar chord)</u>

FRETBOARD PRO
VIDEO COURSE

Here at Acoustia, our programs also include step-by-step video lessons. **You can purchase the follow along video lessons at the following link:**

WWW.ACOUSTIA.COM/FRETBOARD-PRO

ACOUSTIA MERCH

Want to show off your love of guitar to your family and friends? Grab some Acoustia merch. I've always worn these shirts in our instructional videos, and some students have been asking me to release them. **Let me just say...they're super comfy.** You can find some of our merch below:

We're planning to really expand our online store here at Acoustia. Currently our selection is pretty limited, but we are always adding new merch and guitar products. To checkout our online store just click the button above or **click here.**

This is the end of the program for now, although I recommend keeping that momentum going. That's how you'll be successful with guitar in the long run. I really recommend continuing to learn and joining different programs we have here at Acoustia. **Good luck on the rest of your guitar journey!**

Printed in France by Amazon
Brétigny-sur-Orge, FR